Sleeping with the Beloved

Sleeping with the Beloved

108 Writings of Devotion

NICHOLA JOHNSON

Sweet surrender into the night.

Blue black darkness settling over this body, stripping away the unessential.

Toes become ankles before dissolving into hips.

Differentiation of parts from the whole loses its tenure.

Edges blur into something other than the daylight me..

No individual quality....

No tendencies

No needs

No fear

I am sleeping with the Beloved.

Devotion

Devotion 1

Devotion might cost you your life.

For there is no release from the grip
  of just one brush with Bliss.

It permeates the depth of your soul,

Holding you hostage for a trickle of the nectar.

The sweetness an aphrodisiac for the pulse of aliveness.

You sell your sanity in return for the fragrance of ecstasy.

Promising devotion to the gods and goddesses who
  sentry the golden gates to eternity.

Devotion ǐǐ

The driving snow freezes your toes
  and numbs your mind,

I didn't know it could talk...

But I heard the voice echo across the valley,

Clearly beckoning to me...

"Come, Come the purity of the driven snow will sanctify
  you and remove all worry and doubt."

How will I cross this forbidden snow?

"Inure yourself for the journey-the law of longing will
  apply. The mountain carries the pain for those whose
  hearts have bled the wound of devotion."

My Beloved

You are fire for my soul.

A raging inferno of bliss,

Dangerous enough to scorch everything I have come to trust is me.

On what ground will I stand when your breath blows the winds of fire across my life?

When the timbers of my house glow orange red.

When the path that is my life evaporates in front of me.

Where will my heart take refuge?

Where will I bury my singed body?

The Beloved

The Beloved lingers in the shadow.

The place where all manifestation begins.

The darkroom of creation.

Do not try to use your eyes to see the Divine.

They betray the truth.

Your breath must slide under the doorway of light and
   slip into the boundless room of darkness.

There you will inhale yourself into the center of creation
   and exhale the Divine.

Tears splintering into sparks of energy.

Fragments of the Divine scattered
  across the whole of creation.

Bursting into columns of dancing fire.

Waves of daring heat emanating absolution of desire.

In Love with the Divine

You dragged the blue feather across my thigh
  to places unknown.

Where my spirit had frozen in time.

You traced the lines of disappointment across my back
  until they disappeared into the darkness,

Wandering the skies with me in search of moons from
  other galaxies.

You shaded me from the sun's expanding corona with
  your wings of tungsten,

Silvery-grey filigree illuminated by
  exploding supernovas.

Where else would I find unquestionable joy mixed with
  tears of transition?

Why would I travel further for answers
  to questions not asked?

The Beloved II

The beloved is suspended on the edge of my knowing,

Perched upon the branch of shadows.

Neither fully illuminated nor darkened
  by the mask of illusion.

I glance beyond my shoulder, the filtered light capturing

 a slight movement, not measurable by the finite.

I close my eyes in reverence
  and striking brilliance floods my interior.

Words for the Beloved

The tears jut across my cheeks like the shooting stars
   writing upon the new moon sky.

The skipping stones dancing across the pond of illusion

Where they come from, I know not...

The journey they take me on I am beginning to witness.

It is more of a scent than a destination.

An urge to open my heart just a wisp wider,

And the flood of words usher themselves out into the world

Holding their worth in unsubstantial ways.

They are simply one portal to the wholeness of you
   Divine One.

And yet they are like the bud giving birth to its fullness.

They are a manifestation of the embodied form where
   you have graciously placed me.

The capacity to utter a sound which sends a vibration
   across the universe....

Such majesty, such brilliance...as only the Divine can
   truly know.

Words, a meager offering from my heart to my Creator.

The Divine Crept In

I am not burdened by the smallest tear in my heart,

A slipknot hole where you have crept in.

I can not escape the knowing of your presence,

The wash of fullness across my body.

It is a weight to hold the potential of all.....

Or more the potential of nothing.....

Somewhere amidst all and nothing,

the fate of the sacred unfolds.

The Invitation to the Beloved

I invited you to stay for a lifetime,

You only stayed for a fortnight.

Following the cries of longing, you move from one
   encampment to another.

Settling in as the sun sets behind the mountains and the
   cool air moves across the valley,

Chandra rising with great anticipation.

"Why did you leave", I cried....

"I did not leave", you replied, "You gave birth to me,

under the rising moon."

"And so I shall be in and with you always."

"See, you have found me here,
   amongst the cries of anguish~where else would I be?"

Beauty

I am the rose growing in the garden of invitation.

My scent is never denied to those who find it impossible
to pass by me without stopping.

"Lean in," I whisper " for the intensity of me
can not be experienced from afar."

Close you eyes so I might carry you into places without
language,

Where the heart caresses your shadow into the light.

Do not fear my thorns for Love bleeds rich blue red,

In the river of the Divine.

Grace

Whispers of grace.

A hint of the Divine.....

Lingering in the shadow behind the great magnolia tree.

Blossoms begging to burst forth with the fragrance of everlasting life.

An elixir of sweetness and sorrow.

The Sun's warmth casting aside all hesitation.

Twisted Petals unfold with shyness into the glare of the unknown.

I am but a single bud
  waving myself across the valley floor.

Shifting and settling at the whim of the wind.

I have no fiat of self.

No urgings of particular order.

I dance across the tarmac of possibility
  at the request of the Divine...

Releasing my fragrance as it rises
  out of the essence of me...

Reflecting the dew of the breaking morning;

I am the light of transformation.

I am a solitary leaf, dancing on the breath of the Divine.

Skirting here and there with the illusion of randomness.

The brilliance of design not yet visible in my
limited sight.

The Divine sings me the song of surrender.

Each note decreasing my resistance...

Until my lightness of being has no play of its own.

Standing on the pier, scanning the possibilities.

To what depth must one dive
  to encounter the luminous oyster,

Destined to tarry on the ocean floor throughout eternity?

To collect the ultimate gift of radiance and grace?

Offered through abject surrender to the grit of life.

The oyster knows no other manner
  than to blindly create beauty.

Willingness

Tears dripping down my cheeks.....

It isn't enough to shed tears the Divine One said, "They
   must find their way into the depths of the soul and
   purify the path for the embodied ones....

Sprinkle them across the ground so they may
   become glimmers of gold illuminating the path
   of the tender heart,

And the journey of love for others to know that love
   conquers all.

Allow each tear to become a divine dipping pool.

Become submerged in each tear
   and taste the nectar as you are gasping for breath.

Expel your tendencies until the last bit of humanness has
   been driven from your being exposing the
   exquisiteness of the Divine resting in you.

Then my dear one,
   your tears will have found their way home."

I did not know the winds coming from the west would
blow me OVER before I had fully faced the rising sun.

I did not know that rain would wash UP my body spring-
ing from the torrents of water overflowing the basin.

I did not know that I could look through my own eyes
and see the pain you carry even before you know it to
be truth.

I did know that my journey had taken a hairpin turn.

These things have become my new knowing…

You are the untethered feather.

Dancing across the artist's palatte of life.

Cajoling colors into hues of monsoon skies
and naked beaches.

Escaping the downdraft of destiny;

Willingness your billowing sailcloth of potentiality as
you skirt across the sky.

The Rock People

Gaping holes exposing the jagged edges of humanity.

Raw junctures where surfaces are mismatched....unsteady footing.... yet still standing in unclaimed juxtaposition to one another.

Quietly and with steely presence the Divine casts an unceasing stream of sand over the pile.

Divine Grace filling every crevice until the precious holes become the muster for the pile of rocks you call your life.

Sunyata

Shard Slivers

Shard slivers scattered across the ground

Remnants from the illusion of wholeness.

She dances between the sharp edges, pirouetting
   en pointe her diaphanous skirt swirls around her.

Becoming the ocean wave; raising and falling with the
   tide of her intention, crashing into ecstasy.

Faster and faster she twirls as the ocean gives way to the
   breaking dawn of consciousness.

Sun swept shards becoming the path to the Divine.

Are you in my emptiness or my fullness?

Are you the river or the riverbed?

In *Shunya* where the pristine emptiness of the barren
basin dries cracks in the clay form....

Or in *Purna* where the torrential overflowing of the
Ganga ma plunges across the armored banks, washing
out all form.

Dropping form ..

Peeling the skin into raw patches...

Stretching transparency into the voids....

Absence of connected tissue.

Fingers extended into the emptiness.

Fear dancing on the edge of tactile reassurance.

Where there was, there is no longer.

Tears cannot quench the thirst.

The path well traveled.

Littered with impressions of wanderers past tense.

Littered slopes of well tread messiness.

Meandering across uneven terrain.

The inevitable fork.

Risking wholeness against the seed cracked open upon
the edge of a jagged protruding truth.

There is no you.

There is no path.

Where are you?

In silent screams I dance spirals around you.

Casting off entanglements as the sparks of energy
  explode into the darkness.

Tiny fireworks of the heart.

Like fireflies in the night,

Certain to perish in the deepest passage towards the light.

There is no story to tell or truth to live into.

The dawn's light will prove the absence of all.

The Divine Is Looking

The Divine is looking at me
  through the windowpane of love.

The accumulated streaks and dirt
  obscuring the view.

I am still me.

I fling open the window to expose the naked and
  unadorned being I am becoming.

There is nowhere to hide in the moonlit night.

The veneer of humanness
  losing force against the weight of the Divine.

Love yanking the last creeping tendrils
  of stubbornness off the trellis,

Revealing the emptiness of form.

It appears as a deep pool of nothingness.

Blackness masking something more...

Substance is subjective.

Emptiness is objective.

What is relative against the two?

There is a melancholy here for me.

Spirit reaching deep inside
  for an unidentified piece of self.

Sifting grains of sand through bowls of wood.

Emptiness, the caldron of the Divine.

Seeking a vessel in which to hold the formless.

Unbounded holding boundless;

Silence speaking in tongues.

No one hearing the strings plucked in
  a moment of abandon,

A soliloquy to an audience untamed..

In a vacuum... finding you pressed against the fence of
  witness.

Holding the gate open so I could dive into the emptiness!

The Teacher

The Teacher

Your footsteps leave grooves on my heart.

Gouges where the underskirt of my armor has been
scraped away!

The nakedness of spirit stands in exposed relief.

I dare not touch the places of tenderness, for the
floodgate hangs on broken hinges.

A wave of tears will simply wash away all that is me...

Drowned in a perfume of gentle ballads.

And so I patch my heart with rags soaked in holy water
and wait for Revelation.

I am scraping and clawing my way to the Divine.

I do not know if you are a stepping stone or the path.

Whether to skip across you in joy for the
    temporary footing or to surrender the entirety of
    my being to you.

To vacate self and take up domicile in other.

Your face haunts my dreams while your hands
    tenderly wipe my tears, leaving lines of ash across
    my cheeks.

The fire is chasing the root of me.

The place where you have anchored
    the fragrance of the Divine.

Please do not be impatient with me.

My heart has wanderings without destination.

My stirrings create slipknot's out of sweet reason.

My words-twisted carnage for liberation is cunning,

My frailties windows into my soul's desperation.

Sit with me in the changing light of my unfolding.

There is a reasonable chance...

That you will be the fire that consumes the form that I claim as me.

Fanning the flames leaving me as a pile of ashes.

There is a reasonable chance...

That you will be the wind blowing those ashes across the mountains and into the valley.

There is a reasonable chance...

That you will be the sun penetrating the valley floor

Until the ashes, in the sun's inferno, cease to exist.

Teacher

The yearning turns the prayer wheel round and round.

Daring to ask for the sacred blessing.

The baptism of faith, crossing the threshold,

Arriving nowhere but recognizing how far
  I have traveled.

Anticipation trumping trepidation. And yet....

How will teacher show up?

Egoless? Empty? Illimitable?

I open my being to receive the blessing,

Vulnerability spilling over my body and soul.

Crying out for unbounded compassion and
  righteousness,

Teacher heeds the call for accountability and touches me.

With neither the burning of flesh nor the entrapment of
  the mind.

I have been delivered into the arms of the Divine.

Surrender

So many tears flowing into the river.

Stop for a moment and feel them trickling down your
cheeks for they belong not to me nor you.

They are homeless expressions of surrender.

The dew glistened in the early Sun.

Its iridescence magnifying the hidden kernels of knowing and truth.

Tiny fragments strewn across time and eternity.

The darkness having witnessed the translucent nature of the Divine.

Sweet Grace moving as a vapor in and around the slumbering

Taming the face of fear-hovered-wildly awake.

Tenderly rocking the tiniest of creatures into cocoons.

Vessels of perfected emptiness.

Divine Sacred intention stirring the memory of Oneness, leaving a trail of teardrops waiting for dawn's light.

I am in the middle of a dust storm.

My eyes scream for relief from the penetrating needles.

I can not see the path home.

The swirling dust is sandpaper against my skin.

Tearing pieces of my flesh from the bone leaving
   me raw and vulnerable.

Where is the signpost?

If I can not see it will I recognize its fragrance?

The wind is relentless, singing ballads of antiquity as it
   pulls me to the ground.

Prostrate, my arms stretched out in surrender,
   my fingertips graze the signpost hidden beneath
   the dust.

The twig cracked under the weight of my foot.

Splintered pieces that once formed the story of my life
now littering the ground.

Broken and left as kindling for the fire raging in the cave
of my soul.

There is no breath spacious enough...

Shallow packets of air don't reach my fingertips.

Urgency is ruthless....thrusting my lifeless hands into the
bloody interior of who I am,

I desperately search for my heart.

I am a jar of tears,

Held but not contained...

Oozing out through my very pores...

not wanting to be measured by any accounts.

It is not their number but their salinity.

Whether they carry electrical charges into the world of
   form or splash silently onto the fabric of life.

Countless expressions of a heart broken open.

The birdcage has lovely filigreed and rolled ironwork.

There is no confusion for the strength of the bars.

The songbird shares her story of captivity and freedom.

The two are not dissimilar.

The bleeding edge blurs as she trusts the door to remain open while she flings herself in its path.

One might inquire, is her flight into or out of the birdcage?

Timelessness

The swing was suspended over time.

Swaying back and forth through seconds
  as they became minutes.

Never accumulating distinctive passage
  to mark a place here and now.

Her feet dangled into the future
  while she was left waiting...
  waiting for momentum to carry the
  pieces of her life across the valley of destiny.

Tears dripping dew upon the landscape of the heart.

Bleeding tiny love notes and pastel drawings.

Collections of moments locked in memories safe box.

Stretched out of touch.

Just a degree separation from the present moment.

Tears gathering life force becoming the river of destiny.

Holding the heart captive to the passage across time.

Delivering the bloodied heart into the arms of the
  Divine.

Tumbleweed

We are tumbleweed dancing across the tarmac.

Sun kissed tangled pieces of mother nature.

Now stationary in the void.

There is no expectation, no prelude.

Only stillness until there is stillness no more.

Until Divine Creation lifts us across the veil of time

And bounces us into the oncoming draft of spirit.

Splash water on your face little one.

The Divine has opened the curtain.

The sun is shining through.

It is time to wake up your spirit.

Don't hesitate for you will regret the missed moments
of Divine reflection.

Tangled bramble obscures the entry.

Discarded memories building the stairway to heaven.

Brazen affront or sheepish approach yield the same
    results.

Abject sentry.

Absent options, time marches forward.

What is life and what is death?

Where do you draw the curtain,

Across the bow or behind the stern?

ma

Anandamayi Ma

She walks with Grace...tiny bare feet skimming the floors
  surface....floating across the room.

When the pitcher is very full it can spill.

Unintended life force cascading over the edges,

Overflowing onto anyone in its path,
  non-discriminate spillage.

Passing through the vortex, startled by the current.

You must not sleep now, the night is brief.

The pulse is quickening,

The form reducing itself to sheer matter.

The Divine has been summoned and the pitcher
  is replenished.

Barefoot

I am barefoot on the dirt path.

What is the barrier between mother and me?

Dust flies up in a cloud of certainty;

It is inevitable,

The rawness of my feet against the dirt path,
 as my humanity can not be escaped.

I beg for dissolution of the veil guarding mother;

That I might see her in the sharp stones
 puncturing the soles of my feet,

Causing me to fall to my knees in utter joy and devotion.

Tears watering the seeds of spirit as I bow down,

Forehead to the earth, praying faith.

Ma's Tears

Ma holds the handkerchief delicately as she spreads it
across the altar in remembrance of the silent tears she
has shed for her children.

Each tear holding the vastness of oceans and the rawness
of broken hearts cracking open.

She has witnessed each tear as a brilliant stone tossed
across the handkerchief with great abandon;

For she knows the jewels of the heart are birthed when
the fire of life exceeds all knowing.

Ganga Ma

I am a stick floating on the mother.

I am a broken piece -having fallen away from the whole.

She does not care.

She only knows the entirety of existence.

She does not see separation.

She experiences me as the sway of spirit
   within the expanse of the cosmos.

I am a shooting star dancing on the reflection
   of mankind.

I am the ONE splintered into facets of brilliance
   lighting the way for the boats carrying
   the dead to their pyre and into eternity.

Jai Ma

She travels with me in curious ways.

The swell of a wave across the shore of my heart.

The whisper of her name upon my lips captures the
impermanence of the wave.

She chases me out of the temple and into the sanctuary
of my heart.

Tears springing joyfully from the well of thirstlessness.

Gratitude becomes a fragrance I drown myself in.

Swaha Om Jai Ma, I weep for her presence.

Offering oblations for the soul,

Remembering that I am but a tributary in the flow of
mankind destined to empty into the Divine.

The Divine Mother

The beloved enters the room wearing the
  cloak of humanity,

Showing up as the simplest of creatures.

Unadorned and undiscovered she plants
  the seeds for the unfurling.

You are caught in the indescribable spiral of creation
  And the unfolding of Grace.

Your deepest self greets the Beloved
  with recognition and delight.

The Lila has begun.

Anandamayi Ma

Daily tears spill over on her behalf.

I know her as my sleeping self.

I brush against the edge of her skirt
  while wandering the path.

She reaches out and grasps my hand.

Eyes demanding my full surrender.

Her slight head tilt reassures me that she is with me

And yet I ache from loneliness.

Where was I when her form graced this world?

Why was I not called to sit at her feet
  and be caressed by her smile?

Motherhood

...Motherhood is dripping honey from the spoon of
holes,

Where our heart leaks compassion and joy,
while knowing tears and loneliness.

She waits patiently while the stickiness of life
melts into the sweetness of the nectar and ushers
her into bliss.

Jai Ma Devi

I approach her with trepidation.

We have been separated by responsibility.

Not for absence of devotion.

Lifting the raw silk veil my heart pauses..
  Is my presence still familiar?

Will she allow my tears to wash across the gulf between
  the embodied and spirit?

Gingerly I place my hands just above the form of her,
  hovering momentarily before entering
  the temple of the consecrated.

My body moves in response to Her call
  to deepen into the Unknown She.

I lose the world of words and sink into timelessness.

She pulls my hands to her bosom and embraces me.

MA

I know she's with me My dearest Ma,

Anandamayi Ma.

She sends a shudder through my body to remind me
  of her presence-as though I could forget.

Have I crossed over or am I still lingering on the edge
  between two worlds?

Ego standing as sentry limiting passage
  through the portal between the two,

Promising unfulfilled gifts,

Shiny rings and dangling bracelets catch my eye.

Her barefoot feet and downcast eyes catch my heart.

I feel her shadow holding vigil in the doorway.

The beads of her Mala slipping
  silently through my fingers.

My breath peaceful and silent. Where am I?

Sadhana

The Mala

I hold the prayer mala loosely in my grasp.

Fingers sliding smoothly across the pearls,

Counting silently the many names for God....

The rhythm deepening into the Grace of the Divine.

Eyes scan the inner landscape as the breath slackens.

I am held tenuously between realms.

Shivaya Namah,

Dissolving the bonds which tether me to this body.

The entirely of the cosmos held in suspension between
    this breath and the next.

The pearls slide noiselessly out of my grasp.

Uncounted prayers ignite the internal fire of liberation.

My life becomes the Mala
    pearled into droplets of bliss and joy.

The rains did not come.

Dust storms raged across the prairie of reasonable
   expectation,

Scorching the seedling of hope.

Three Fingers pressing against the open space
   between my brows.

Inhale

yoga yoga yogishwaraya

Exhale

butha butha bhuteshwaraya

Inhale

kala kala kaleshwaraya

Exhale

shiva shiva sarveshwaraya

Torrential downpour.

Flooding across the mountains.

Beads stringing together the sacred and the mundane.

Traversing territory between the seen and the unseen.

Tossing open the windows of fear and dusting off the
patterns of vicissitude.

Painting peace signs across your forehead

As markings for the Divine touch of equanimity.

The Tent and the Altar

I am passing through a green and lush valley with only
  my tent and altar to carry.

Nightly I pitch my tent upon the hallowed
  ground of Spirit.

Raising an altar into the sacred space
  where humanity greets Divinity.

My prayers open the floodgates and ancient ones
  permeate the air around me.

In weighted silence I mark time for the continued
  measure of Presence,

Reclining in deep and penetrating gratitude.

Kumkumam

She extends her bejeweled finger into the copper bowl.

Pressing firmly-the pressure in response to her hunger.

Leaving her fingerprint on the mirror of devotion,

she touches the two white petals of Ajna...

opening the gate to the inner realms.

With the stain of surrender....

connecting the unfurling humanity to the Divine One.

The external mark of homage for an internal reverence.

Words belie the profundity of the splash of color.

To the untrained eye,

Simply a smudge of rouge gone awry,

Not recognizing Shakti rising out and flushing
the deepest truths into the room.

And the outpouring of tears;
the final exquisite response to the handprint of God.

The Puja

The pujari petitions on behalf of the gathered ones.

Invoking the presence of the Divine.

Calling forth a caldron as the repository for the brew of
  Holy Spirit and Divine Inspiration.

She lifts her arms in celebration of the aarti~

The light waved in the darkness~revoking the Ratri...

Illuminating the inner cavern where
  humanity melts into Divinity.

The chanted words an invitation into no-time.

The flowers discharging a fragrance of remembrance
  wafting across the heart, as the revelation of
  purification seeks the highest ground.

The Mind

Life is a rope of knots creating a ladder of illusion.

The places one has been....

The life passages which have been crossed over....

Winding in spirals slipping the rope through to make
another knot.

It is a journey of turnings.

Folding back upon oneself.

1000 steps to nowhere,

In the destiny of faith.

Grasp the rough twinning while the rope shreds the
mind's stubborn insistence on domination.

Everywhere wheels are twisting into abstract spirals.

Holograms of potentiality shifting perspective.

The body witnessing the turning in upon itself.

A Quickening…

Spiraling momentum spinning off accumulated
  layers of rubble.

Flying chunks of calcified humanness;

Releasing the mind into creative splendor.

It is the winter of my soul.

Pristine layers of inaccessible juiciness weighted down
   by nature's resolute that I be still.

Under the blanket of surrender,

The Divine tends the fire of intention.

Scorching my restless mind.

Blurring the distinction between discrete and collective.

Any perceptible movement marring the peace and
   leaving footsteps leading nowhere.

The Mind

The minds entanglement knows no end.

Cocooned in a well dressed tourniquet proposing
  carefully crafted thoughts.

Truth held hostage in the vernacular of the erudite.

Breath withheld to sustain the moment of inaccuracy.

It is just that it's child's play
  pulling out the most colorful block,

Watching the leaning tower finally collapse.

Ribbons of paint expressing themselves as tears
   sliding down the mirror.

You were not present to witness the reflection.

Eyes peering out, layered behind the streaks.

What is truth and what is suggestion?

Waves of silver distort the value and perception.

It is all in the mind's eye.

A swipe of the sweater covered fist across the mirror
   does not remove the tears.

Is it truth or suggestion?

Silence

The Silence

The silence was deafening.

This body had to cover its ears to stop
   the scream of quietude.

The pool of silence had no surface and no bottom.

Darkness enveloped the entirety of its volume.

This body knew no boundaries -meeting self as other.

Meeting silence as truth.

The silent pool...

Evanescence of body and tanglings,

Lifted across the veil in dissolving chunks of humanness.

Slighter ever so, lighter ever more.

It is you as the pool..

Nearer to you than my breath.

Closer to you than my own hands and feet.

I am drowning in the enormity of nothingness.

Silence dripping off of me.

Pondering silence in its many forms....

Best kept silence is the secret of nature's unrequited love
    for man.

Cajoling humanity from dawn to dusk.

Painterly strokes of well placed hues transcending all
    imagination.

Attempting to seduce just one busy mind with
    the solitude of the Hansa Rugosa.

Come, wither with me into seeds of hope.

Trail down the creek into prickly bramble.

Toss noisy thoughts into the foam of my raging river.

Sacrifice yourself into the arms of my deepest valley.

Surely my tears for you shall slide down your face in
    rivulets of wonder.

I am alone in the house of silence.

Voices of yesteryear whisper

In a language only my bones can hear.

Windows watching for trespassers delirious as to tread
across the threshold.

Steps alerted to the weight of nothingness.

Who dares to enter that which is not...

To relinquish self into the abyss of emptiness...

Waiting for the Divine

Longing demanding attention.

Formless tears occupying the cavity of being.

Expanding into spaces unrevealed.

Ceaseless memories dancing along the string of legacy.

Shadows of knowing…insulting the thinking mind.

Dragging sensibility sideways into the glare of fear.

There is no arrival short of departure from expectation.

Prophecy sits upon the lips of heretics.

Halt all meaningless noise; repose in silence.

Om Namah Shivaya

Om Namah Shivaya

I am slipping into the pool of illusion.

Footing unstable on the moss covered rocks.

Dark shadows create chapters in the story of need.

Layering panic upon fear, creating judgement.

Om moves Divine light through my body

Namah calls my spirit back to truth.

Shivaya releases me from the talons of the mind.

I am at Peace.

The Bridge

I am suspended over a deep crevice.

Narrow and unprotected the bridge sways with spirit.

Jagged rocks below reveal themselves
    as the moon traverses the sky.

I close my eyes.

One foot delicately placed in front of the other.

Heel first.

Toes following one at a time.

Intention.

Silence summons the teacher within.

She speaks in tongues of ancient knowing.

The sounds guide my body.

Shambhoo.

The bridge begins to fade,

this body is suspended only by that which is truth.

There is no form.

There is only spirit and she sings me home.

Clouds

Amorphous shape shifting.

Sky projections of Absolute Truth.

Absent fiat of meager desire.

Relative movement, the illusion continues.

Drift with me into the masked horizon of limitation.

We can not be stopped for the curtain parts
  as the tears of recognition flow.

Wings lifting into the unknown.

Feathers singed by the heat of reality.

Absent the shattered filter of avoidance.

Present the gritty light of absolute presence.

You can't turn the prayer wheel without dropping the weight of prohibition.

Sink into the chant of shiva for the falling gives way to the rising.

Bartering tears for grains of sand.

Building you a temple of devotion upon
  the beach of longing.

Tear by tear, grain by grain…inimitable temple.

An illusion of form and function;

Breached by the vagaries of life.

Yet, withstanding all blustering winds
  and relentless waves,

Passing the torch of love across its threshold,

Fortifying absolute presence.

The heart empties out its sorrow
  into the rising temple of truth.

Trust

The Unraveling

The threads are unraveling.

Colorful snips and pieces of your life lying
 carelessly on the floor.

Your eyes scan the messy fragments of your story.

How is one to separate the wheat from the shaft?

Spirit cries tears for the words which can not be spoken,

Dripping off your chin in rivulets,

Of gold and myrrh.

Priceless reminders for the legacy of form.

Your delicate hands reach down to gather
 that which is left,

Cradling the memories which will stitch
 your life back together.

There is hope.

The earth-moist and receptive.

The rains having washed away all resistance.

The early morning sun penetrating the surface
and loosening the top layer of debris,

Exposing the compost of lifetimes beneath.

Fertile and willing, the seeds risk the unknown as they
stretch towards the light.

The Untethered Heart

Freedom is a knife of sorts.

It cuts away the tangled edges of our mind's eye.

The places where we have become
   encumbered by ourselves.

Where the weight of our thoughts has collapsed the
   perfection of the heart.

The heart must be left to soar beyond the limitations

Of thought and dance with the stars.

It must brush with the fire of renewal in every second

And be born again to the majesty of "I Am".

It must soar untethered into places unseen

With destinations unknown so that the order of the uni-
   verse is held in sacred Suspension.

Stretching trust

I am the impatient archer.

Arrows straying, anchoring into the untamed horse.

Wildly dragging me into the desert of my soul.

Absence of safety or reason.

Mind racing, grasping at disparate pieces of my story.

Horse, no thoughts, head down, drives deeper into the desert.

Thirst of the ridden and the rider recede under the call of the unbridled.

Must stay on now, falling off sure death.

One last glance over my shoulder..the mirage fading away.

Only trust remains.

The ocean of bliss

I can not locate myself within it.

There are no reference points.

I float, I sink, I rise up to the wave
that sweeps through and around me,

Exposing the fragile edges of humanity
I call me.

Wave after wave wearing down my identity.

Inviting me to take the risk..becoming small in return
for infinite possibility.

Turning to Embrace the next set of waves,

Abandoning all

I dive blindly into the surf and find I
am Home.

Leap

The heart is but a seed to be cracked
upon the rocks of fearlessness.

Daring to bleed to death-giving birth to timelessness.

Close your eyes and leap into the abyss for your spirit
has the wings of angels.

Redemption

The angel of death holds the chalice full to overflowing.

The eons of rubbish layered unevenly
  creating an imbalance.

The tipping point finding its roots in the story of that
  which is not.

Truth unwilling to share the cup of redemption while the
  tears of choice water the compost of the heart.

Lila

Lila

The words bubble up from the stream of consciousness,

Where you and I play on the banks of the ganga ma-

Tossing stones and watching ripples becoming words.

In our lila we spin straw into gold, and dance...

A pocketful of posies, upstairs, downstairs,
  we both fall down.

I practice tapas while you wander the skies.

As you are absent, so is the divine collaboration.

The edges of your silence create a vacuity
  in my souls voice.

From the shadow of Mount Kailash you summons me
  to remember my nature.

Pyramid mountain.

Stepping its way into the heavens.

On the precipice of nothingness...

Arms flung open to witness the fall.

Falling up...

Jagged edges poking holes on the ascent.

Torrid sun blaze burning layers of skin.

Fingernails digging into crevices of memory.

No footing for the embodied ones.

Passage impossible.

Form must disintegrate under pressure of spirit.

The Horizon

The horizon of awareness reaching her hand across dimensions.

Beckoning me to fall into her trance.

Tempting me with colors the hue of God's utterances.

Layers of light refracted through the tunnel of Grace.

Dawn and dusk riding on the tight wire of objet indifference.

Slipping out of my skin I surrender the tether of humanity and walk the wire towards the light.

-

Life, the canvas of the soul.

At one time virgin purity,

Stark emptiness, void of reflection for absolute
absorption.

Indifferent to outcome, layers of painterly isolation
accrue.

Color and texture spilling over the edges.

Bleeding okra into plum and black into gray.

Reflection becoming the leela of life-tossing colors back
into the playground of vigilant seekers.

My shadow dances across the mountain ridge.

An imperceptible shape against the jagged rocks.

Sharply I pull it back,
  stitching it to the bloodied surface of my heart.

The dark night my companion,

the moon barely catching my reflection
  in places it is lapsed to travel.

I sink on bruised knees,

Listening as the mountain chants tears of
  Divine presence,

Unraveling the threads of bondage through resonate
  cries of hope.

Liberation

Dawn

The dawn is of sunlight and horizons of the soul.

Windows flying open. ...

Curtains ripped from the rod....

Revealing the bird nest in the barren tree having survived
the harsh winter.

Footsteps on the grass path weaving their way towards
nothingness disappear out of sight
as the dew evaporates into the sunlight.

I wait patiently for the sun to fully rise on my soul and
give light (birth) to the universe.

The Veil of Encumbrance

She wears the veil across her head and shoulders.

Covering her face, she hides the shame of her ancestors.

The veil of secrecy camouflaging the places in her she
  denies.

Bracing herself against the penetrating judgements
  and assessments of her own life.

She moves with footsteps informed by the density of that
  fabric in her life,

Halting her freedom to embody her true nature.

The veil is a temporal condition,

Mediating between the shadow of legacy
  and the expression of reality.

It can be removed at any juncture where the heart meets
  itself.

The Veil of Liberation

The veil ripped as the curtain between earth and heaven dissolved.

Exposing the vast valley of desire and intention to be at one with creation.

She gently drapes the ripped veil across her shoulders as she enters the temple of her soul, meeting Grace and truth.

She smiles as she crosses the threshold of remembrance and embraces the Absolute.

The veil guarding the gate to the temple as she sinks into bliss and merges with herself.

∞

Sometimes the heart travels in spaciousness,

Migrating over long distances.

Butterfly wings trusting spirits intelligence in harmony
 with truth.

Silently the butterfly flies into the unknown,
 seeing beyond the apparent...

Ultraviolet brilliance cascading over its wings.

Sometimes the heart struggles to move
 gracefully across the horizon.

The binding of the chrysalis impeding movement.

Nothing to do but wait for the metamorphosis
 is in God's hands.

Love

How deep Is the Cavern of my Heart?

When did discrete desire become ruthless longing?

The precise moment when I screamed in despair for the love lost while I had toiled in the waiting. ...

Not tasting the eternal moment of my Beloved,

Reflected in the bottomless pool of my tears...

Not daring to breathe the endless breath of fusion

Between longing and love.

The heart weeps its own story.

Stranded on pristine blankets of snow crested mountains.

Drowning on sand drenched beaches in far away dreams.

Reason withstanding...

The mind's eye detouring sensibility,

To embrace just one second of love.

The sun in rising on the totality of humanity.

Droplets of singleness,

Dissolving into a vastness of the One.

Boundaries of ego reluctantly relinquishing footing,

While Love vanquishes all tendencies.

The sun rises on love.

Soft whispers from the night

having woven desire and hope into ribbons;
  bindings for the heart.

Invisible until the indecencies of life
  tear at the fiber of your love.

When your heart cracks apart like the coconut offering
  for the fullness of Chandra.

When the tears you shed drench all that is your life.

Then my dear one, the bindings you have tenderly woven
  press against the entirety of your body and his.

Stretched until the knots bind into eternity.

It is not possible to measure the strength
  of a mother's arms...

For they were formed from God's eyelashes;

Dropping silently through eternity as he cries tears of
  compassion for the journey he knows she
  must undertake.

For the depths she must fall to catch her children before
  touching the edge.

For the wandering she must survive
  without knowing the truth.

The Beloved bows to the darkness necessary to
  illuminate the Love in a mother's heart.

◈

Lightness of Being

The Closed Window

The window closed but the curtain remained open.

Her life narrative reduced to a flimsy piece of fabric,

In the aftermath of the surging winds which had given
   birth to an altered reality.

Layers of recurrence, flung aside,
   unnecessary padding discarded.

The offending weight a burden she no longer needed to
   protect herself.

Raw and naked, she wandered the room

Seeking solace from any negligible sign.

Her gaze lit upon the panel of fabric,
   floating across the closed window

And she rested her head against the painted sash
   remembering her Lightness of Being.

The Garden of Abundance or Despair?

The darkness is a cloak over the garden,
  The Garden of Abundance or Despair?

She tiptoes on the path of filtered shadows
  illuminating her steps.

Brambles reach out to hold her back, struggling against
  the thorns tearing her delicate skin into rivers of red.

She searches for the altar of weights and measures where all
  manifestations are arbitrated against the unseen sacred.

How will her collection of baubles and bricks be judged?

She stumbles into the clearing of rose-gold light and falls
  onto her knees.

In reverence she offers her most precious gift,

Her transcendent purity, her deep comprehension of the
  innate perfection and beauty in all of creation.

She lays a gold and jeweled package upon the altar,

Dipping her fingers into the honey of inner abundance
  and smiles as the Lotus flower unfolds to greet her.

Tears

Filling the bucket with tears.

Sliding noiselessly across her cheeks until they form
a stain of red.

She knows the source and weeps for the
tenderness of the offering.

When the heart cracks it knows no bounds.

The bucket must withstand the flood.

Truth

The winds of truth whistled through
  the valley of discretion.

Revealing only the desired kernels of absolute.

How does outcome wrestle with partial truth?

Layers of storytelling spun into fairy tales.

Becoming truth without a backwards glance.

With the neatness of a dagger you trim away the excess
  exposing only truth.

God's House

God's house has no roof.

The sun burns the torn edges of the book of Sutras
 lying on the weathered farm table.

Pages flipping forward in time as the breeze caresses
 the table.

The rains cross the horizon,

Washing the sins of the forlorn into the stream of
 redemption.

The stillness slowing humanity's breath until
 Peace prevails.

Death

-

Î Am Ƥracticing Death Today

I am on the threshold of dying;

Practicing my death each day now.

Perched on the edge of the Hoop of Fire...

Peering into the burning horizon of those brave enough
   to sacrifice the known for the promised.

Scorching the edges of life's entangled ways.

Unwinding the story of false self.

Dying over and over again.

Until the practiced death midwives the unbounded birth.

Death

It is possible to love so completely
    that death ceases to exist?

The entanglements of physicality dropping away?

The markers of beginning and
    end dissolving into eternity.

Blurred edges erased…chalk on a blackboard
    disappearing.

Pain swept into the dustbin.

Nothing left to arbitrate.

Nothing to bump up against…no reference point to
    defend.

The heart transcends space and time,

Waking the sleeping giant
    who opens the gate to deathlessness.

Fear

Fear...a sweeping brush fire

Consumption its only desire

Purging the earth beneath your feet

Showing no mercy for truth

Escaping its grip... the mantra of the heart belying the sweetest revenge..the fire of fear illuminating the tender seedlings of consciousness unwilling to succumb...

Reaching into tomorrow.

Are not the sunset, as the culmination of light, and

death as the culmination of LIFE, both moving our
hearts in the same way?

Sunset of life; the head of sleeplessness lies upon the
shadow of death,

Ghostly feet wearily pacing the worn wooden floors.

Searching the annals for cracks in memories safe.

Deeply grooved patterns releasing vapor streams of
denial…

Until at last, unhinged humanness initiates dissolution.

Approaching Death

The edges are blurring.

The space between life and death no longer
  gathering moss.

A hundred shades of gray dissolve as the curtain is
  ripped from the rod of regret revealing a thousand
  shades of white.

No backward glance permitted.

She and I, we are falling into the emptiness.

Form releasing the fragrance of the bittersweet.

She lays her head in my lap
  while my tears erase the pain from her face.

A million shades of iridescence.

Death...

Lingering by the doorway.

Testing the limits of recognition.

Twisting the doorknob with bloodless guile.

Silently entering the cavern of consciousness....
　You are sleepwalking..

An unfurling of abject negotiation with the Divine...
　to no avail.

The instantaneous knowing that held
　in every second is a death.

More tragic than death itself if you do not become alive
　to it in the moment.

Shadow

The shadow projects out in front of me;

A needle darning the stretched edges to my physicality.

There is no way around it, the path rambles through it.

I hesitate...

The shadow moves ever so slightly,

The sun gently traversing the sky.

I chase it into the seed of me.

The embryonic part of me which is covered
  by my life story.

It fashions a spotlight upon the frailties of my life.

In juxtaposition, it illuminates the places of brokenness
  and fear.

Opportunities to burn through stickiness.

In its depth, breadth and width, I cannot contain the
  whole if it;

My inner light must dissolve its own shadow,

Or dance in the darkness forever.

The Guru's Chair

The chair is empty....of form...

I rattle around the perimeter testing
   the honesty of the myth.

Is this the spring of revelation or the
   winter of barren presence?

Fragrance of truth or scent of illusion?

Are you sitting or standing as a witness to my faith?

Whose voice is trembling cords of melody; undertones
   of promise?

About the Author

Nichola Johnson is an interfaith minister living in northern California. She founded and guides a spiritual community where she shares the spirit journey of the embodied soul.

She can be found at www.sharedwisdom.org.

Acknowledgements

Nichola thanks her family for their patience and support as she has walked the tangled path of one drawn to the Beloved. She is especially grateful to her husband, Craig, who has given her the gift of freedom and unconditional love. The spiritual path is often obscured from sight. Deep gratitude for the teachers who have offered patience, guidance and illumination for this journey. Finally, a huge thank you to Claire Vaccaro for her support and editing talents. This project would not have manifested without her steady guidance.

About the Illustrators

SAGE KURNIE is a young artist from the Bay Area of California. She started drawing and painting in early elementary school, and since then, she has developed a strong passion for art. Her favorite subjects are nature, people, and animals, and she works with a variety of different mediums, including oil, acrylic, ink, and watercolor.

Sage draws much inspiration from the emotions and interactions she experiences and observes, and tries to capture such feelings in her artwork. Currently in her freshman year as an undergraduate at the University of California, Berkeley, Sage plans to major in Environmental Science or Astrophysics, with either a minor or double major in Art Practice. She looks forward to wherever her artistic journey will take her.

REBEKAH RACHEL JOSEPH is an artist born and living in London. Rebekah studied illustration at the University for the Creative Arts in Farnham. She is inspired by gestural marks similar to calligraphy writing, capturing her drawings through instincts and energy. Rebekah studied illustration at the University for the Creative Arts in Farnham. She is inspired by gestural marks similar to calligraphy writing, capturing her drawings through instincts and energy. Rebekah contributed four illustrations to this project.

Made in the USA
San Bernardino, CA
19 September 2016